YOU ARE LUMINOUS

Homecoming

A collection of encouraging quotes that will help re-empower you
to see the light in all of creation and the beauty in your becoming.

KRISTEN CSUHRAN

DEDICATION

To you: *The one coming back home.*

May you always remember the strength that you carry to overcome.
Of your capability to see love in all of creation.
Of the peace that comes from choosing to be in harmony with the
flow of life.
And may you remember that the Divine is awake and aware in every
part of you always guiding you back to the light.

CONTENTS

ACKNOWLEDGMENTS

To all those who have served my journey in any capacity, whether through love, unconditional support, lessons, tests, or triggers.
Thank you for being my greatest teachers and a mirror into more of myself.
Thank you for showing up to assist my self-mastery and to help encourage me both consciously and unconsciously to step into all I came here to be.

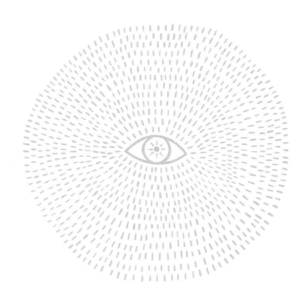

INTRO

I created this book to support you as you walk through the stages of
growth and becoming, guiding you and carrying you with every breath
to see your journey, your lessons, your growing pains all as a gift...
a gift that was so lovingly sent on your behalf as a portal back into
your sovereignty.
When we're centered in our soul and aligned with our heart, we then
merge effortlessly back into harmony with creation, which allows each
step to feel more like grace.
And finally, to remind you of your potential to rewrite the rest of your story
exactly how you'd like it to be.

As you return home to your divinity, first you must release and <u>let go</u> of
the old stories, programs, patterns, density, and false beliefs that are
keeping you small, in a life less than what you're worthy of.
Calling on <u>faith</u> helps you surrender to the unfolding and allows it to be
easier to trust in all you're being called to let go of so that you can
embrace the new birthing through you. Now that you've accepted more is
calling your name, and you honor what's playing out, you naturally begin to
<u>align</u> with a new potential.

Then comes the time where you're given invitations to <u>remember
your power</u> to rewrite your journey and consciously choose
to manifest all that you desire.

And finally, you <u>become.</u>
This is your homecoming..

LETTING GO

In order to begin again and to claim another level of ourselves,
we have to let go of all that is no longer serving our highest
path, purest embodiment, and desired future potential.
We have to unlearn to relearn.
Give to receive.
Cleanse to reintegrate.

The key to letting go is allowance and trust.
It's surrendering to a path ahead that could serve us even
higher than the one we're on now.

It's giving ourselves permission to create space for something
new and having faith that a more bountiful and aligned journey
is ready and on its way to meet us.

RIGHT NOW
YOU'RE BEING
ASKED to CREATE
WIDE OPEN
SPACE
for the
DIVINE
to once again
REACH YOU

Be grateful for everything releasing
from your life right now,
your soul is making way
for greater things.

What if loss's only job was to make space for more:
Gain
Potential
Abundance
Opportunity
Prosperity
Freedom
Light.

Not everything is supposed to stay together.
E x p a n s i o n only occurs in the
o p e n i n g up,
the falling apart,
the surrender,
the softening and unfolding.

Let the universe unravel and take back
that which is no longer meant for you.

Embrace the space for
new potential
and healing to pour in.

The letting go,
ending,
destruction,
and everything known being burned to the ground
was actually to serve the new being you're now ready to embody,
the new abundance you're ready to allow in,
the new freedom to connect you with your infinite potential,
the new dimensions you're about to rise and meet,
the new purpose you're about to merge with,
a new season you're about to master.

Remember that nothing new can enter without something else
releasing to create the space for it.

Endings are a gift.
Endings are always a portal
to more of Divine you...
to the next level of your worthiness.

And then one day you're finally f r e e
because you had the courage all of those times
to let go of what was too small for you,
of what was repressing your heart,
of the patterns that felt comfortable,
but weren't allowing you to fully rise
and meet all that you are.

Be so proud of yourself
for making room
for the next level of you to reemerge,
for your cells to wake back up
and come alive with the glory of what you've finally
honored that you deserve to receive.

Detach from what was, so what is supposed to be
can effortlessly, finally, be.

Let what's served its purpose move on.
Let things come and let things go
with trust,
with surrender,
with a heart wide open.
Something new will always rush back to you
once you've allowed the space for it
and it will always be in more resonance
than what was before it.
Every higher level
is always matched with even higher blessings.

The best hasn't even happened yet.

You naturally realign
with the things that are meant for you
when you let go of what isn't serving you.

All you need to do to let your soul know
you're ready to realign with your blessings
is to let go of what is less than
you're truly worthy of.
That's all.
The Universe will take care of the what, the who,
the when, and the how,
especially the how,
it's infinite after all.
And the why... the why is you were born deserving.
Born worthy.
Your blessings have always been yours.
You've just stopped allowing them all
to reach you by holding other vibrations in their place,
which caused the misalignment.
Let go now so you can rise and meet the light;
so that you can meet your true self.

FAITH

Faith allows us to surrender to the Divine, to our infinite self. It allows us to view our journey, our lessons, our growth with grace and understanding instead of resistance so that we're flowing with the current vs. swimming against it.
It helps us stay in our heart, in trusting what's playing out before us, instead of diving into fear.
It encourages us to honor that our soul has a larger plan for us beyond what we're sometimes able to see on the physical plane and that it's orchestrated each and every moment so perfectly for who we are destined to become at the highest level.

Faith always brings us back to our higher self,
our true nature,

back to the heart.

DON'T WORRY
YOU'RE ON THE RIGHT PATH
YOUR DIVINE PLAN IS UNFOLDING
YOUR MIRACLES ARE COMING
YOU ARE GROWING
IT'S ALL WORTH IT

Just because you don't have it right now
doesn't mean it isn't coming.
And just because it hasn't manifested yet
doesn't mean it's not on its way to you.

Trust in the power you carry to create all you're deserving of.
Trust that everything you've been affirming is already in the process
of manifesting.
Trust you're worthy of receiving it all and more.
Trust that your soul knows exactly when to deliver it to you.

Your soul has the most beautiful plan for you.
Allow it to unfold in Divine timing.

You cannot rush magic.

Relax, your dreams are already in the process of coming true.

What if the only thing you needed to do
to magnetize your dreams to you
was just to have faith that they're already coming true,
that they're in the unseen already taking physical form,
picking out the perfect time to bless you and surprise you.
They're arranging themselves in a way that
will make you more joyful than ever before
because that's the truth.
That's already happening.
Life is always on your side,
but every time you doubt creation,
you doubt your power,
or you doubt your worth,
you block them and they have a harder time finding you.
You literally stand in the way of your own blessings.
So let your armor down and let them finally reach you!
Your belief is the bridge.
By divine birthright,
they're already yours!
Let them come to you!

Maybe you're not being rejected or left behind,
neglected or stuck.
Maybe something even more bountiful,
blissful,
and effortless is on its way to you.
Start believing in your true worth
and the magic of this universe more
and watch all of the ways in which everything conspires in your
highest favor.
Watch all the miracles that show up,
that have actually been surrounding you all along,
waiting for you to wake up
and notice them.
You've got to believe it to see it and receive it, my love.

Be grateful for your blessings in disguise,
for all of the times you didn't get what you wanted
because your soul saw something you couldn't see,
for all of the things granting you miracles
even though they might physically feel like
pain, heartache, or loss.

It's not working out
because something even better
is on its way.
Trust in this divine unfolding.

Maybe the road you're being led down now
takes more time to build
because it's being so perfectly designed
for your highest.
Maybe your blessings to come
are so large they can't all manifest overnight.
Maybe there's a time in the near future
that's so divinely designed
for it all to arrive into your life
and if it came a second sooner
it might not be able to give you
the true abundance you're worthy of.
Just be patient, beloved.
And don't stop believing in the goodness
that is yours to receive.
Your time is coming.

You deserve it all.

Embrace the confusion - the solution will present itself when the timing is perfect.

Embrace the moments of uncertainty - divine direction will guide you when it's safest for you to move and choose something new.

Embrace the isolation - you're growing stronger in your own being and discovering the beauty of who you innately are.

Embrace the ache - it's teaching you about the power of your own love to carry you back to wholeness.

It's all perfect.

Embrace every season of your becoming.

Just because it's not your time yet,
doesn't mean it won't ever be.
These things you're working through,
what you're healing right now,
is getting you closer to your homecoming.
There's a sacred purpose for your being.
And there's a perfect time for all things under heaven.

You have not been forgotten.
Everything happens in divine order.
Trust in the magic coming.
Trust in the process.
Trust in the timing.
Your soul would never forsake you.
It wants nothing more
than to carry you back to abundance.

Right now
you're being prepared for a calling
that is far greater
than you can even imagine.

What if for a second you believed
that nothing could go wrong.
That nothing is wrong.
That you're exactly where you're meant to be.
That this state you're in was divinely designed.
That each and every moment you were supported infinitely.
That everything that comes into your life
is there for you:
as a gift,
to learn,
to ascend,
to appreciate,
to embrace.
That each pain was a blessing.
Each heartache, a miracle.
Each fear, a friend.
Each loss, a strength.
Now keep believing,
because it's true.

But what if your dreams do come true?
What if it all does work out?
What if it's better than you imagined?

What if this is exactly what your soul needs to strengthen and make the rest of your life that much easier?

What if this connection actually didn't serve your highest and now you're finally set free to receive better?

What if losing this just created space for you to actually manifest your true abundance?

What if the best is still yet to come?

What if this just rerouted you onto a path that was even more graceful and beautiful than you could have imagined for yourself?

Everything that you're going through is preparing you for your highest destiny.

This has all been sent on behalf of love for a vision,
a purpose, a plan so much larger than
your human self can even possibly comprehend.
Your soul scripted this journey long before you entered this body
to gift you with light,
grace,
and creation
only you can authentically bring.
It's asking you now to return to your purity,
your home.
Guiding you into remembrance with each lesson
and wound that's coming up for healing.
Returning you back to that innate truth
that lies within your heart.
Those perfect gifts you have always had within you.
Trust in the unfolding,
the growing pains,
the fear with letting go.
Surrender to the release that's taking place
so that new worlds can be birthed in their place.
Have faith in the unseen
always supporting you
and holding you in its embrace.
Be gentle and kind as you continue expanding,
rising,
and becoming.

What's yours has no expiration date.
Your heart is already carrying you there.
All of these lessons are simply steps on the path.

You'll get to where you're supposed to be exactly when you're
supposed to be there.
Trust in the new foundations you're being called to create
with each wound you clear,
which is giving your roots
more stability and strength.
Trust the darkness rising
to amplify your light.
Trust the divine plan your soul laid out for you lifetimes ago.
This is all happening exactly how it should in the unseen.
Merge back with harmony and trust.
Your heart knows the way.

Your wish has already been granted.
Everything you want to be you already are.
Everything you could ever need
is already inside of you.
Everything you desire is innately yours.

IT WILL WORK OUT
IT WILL FLOW WITH EASE
IT WILL FEEL EFFORTLESS

BELIEVE

THIS IS YOUR DIVINE
BIRTHRIGHT

ALIGNMENT

Alignment oftentimes looks like misalignment on the physical plane, so instead of seeing the light, we tend to get caught up in our emotions and feelings of discordance and embody the fear that can come with change. When things show up that appear to be moving us backwards physically, spiritually and energetically, the opposite is always happening.

New beginnings look like endings.
Light looks like darkness.
Wins look like losses.
Harmony looks like discordance.
Freedom looks like isolation.
Balance looks like imbalance.
Breakthroughs look like breakdowns.

But truly, you can never lose or go "wrong" on your journey. There aren't any mistakes, especially when you're very essence is love. You can only ever grow and return back to who you divinely are, despite whatever illusion feels present. So, keep remembering that those "tough places" are really just opportunities for expansion and realignments with something, someone or a new path your soul knows will serve you even higher.

More

Alignment that fulfills you
Connection that supports you
Boundaries that honor you
Voice that empowers you
Heart that softens you
Movement that strengthens you

Maybe that isn't really an obstacle.
Maybe it's a portal of self-discovery,
an opportunity for realignment,
an invitation for freedom,
encouragement to reclaim your highest potential,
the door to a new,
more bountiful path,
a chance to start over.

This is all here on behalf of your highest.
The universe wants nothing more than for you to succeed.

That roadblock,
detour
delay
postpone
obstacle
change in direction
are all actually saving you from a life
that is less than what you're worthy of.

Divine intervention can take on many
names and forms,
but it has only one intention and purpose,
to always carry you even higher,
serve you even better,
and align you with more.

You're not being rejected,
you're being protected
and that requires redirection.

It's not that you weren't worthy enough,
it's that you were worthy of more.
Your soul saw something you couldn't see
and stepped in to save you from a connection,
a life,
that was less than what you deserved.

STOP CHASING
WHAT YOU DESIRE.
RETURN TO
LIGHT AND LET
IT START
CHASING YOU.

When something stops working,
it's because something else is trying to reach you.

Honor the discordance and discomfort
that precedes realignment.
It's simply your intuition
trying to tell you you're ready for more
and gently pushing you there.
Your soul is trying to gift you with signs
to show you and help you
feel what is no longer
in highest resonance with you.
It's time for you to receive something else
that will gift you with even more.

Instead of looking at this as an ending,
try embracing this as the beginning to every dream
you've ever wanted to live.
You're not being destroyed,
left behind,
or broken,
you're being reborn;
brighter, fuller, more luminous.

Sometimes it's just not supposed to work out,
so maybe,
my love,
this new path
you're being redirected to
is the path
you were meant to be on all along.
Release your grip,

s u r r e n d e r.

EMPOWERMENT

Our highest calling is to remember who we truly are. That we are an energetic being who is comprised of infinite potential, innate worthiness, endless resilience and courage. That we always have a choice over what we choose to give life to and that which will manifest in our future. We are ultimately in control of our reality and all that will meet our future self.

As we walk along our journey here, we're given endless invitations to reclaim this power that has always been ours. That we are, by divine birthright, entitled to heal, to awaken, to cultivate more love within and without, and most importantly to finish writing our story the way we absolutely desire it to be.

So, give birth to every divine purpose placed in your heart and embody everything you were created to be.
You are worthy.

You are the one you have been seeking.

No one can heal you the way you can heal you.
No one can love you the way you can love you.
No one can see you the way you can see you.
No one can fully show up to support you the way you can support
you.
No one can nurture you the way you can nurture you.

This is the magic of you.

YOU and YOU
ALONE
are in control of your
DESTINY

This is self-mastery...
That no matter what shows up
and no matter what form it shows up in
you still choose gratitude,
you honor it,
you learn from it
and you allow it to be something that improves you,
not keeps you stuck in a cycle that is no longer serving you.

The Practice
Soul work
Self-mastery
Alchemy
Transmutation....
call it whatever you'd like,
but this is the only way you reclaim your power.
You ascend and rewrite what is no longer serving you
by honoring everything that shows up on your path
like it was sent by the holiest hands
and allow yourself to see the specks of gold in it.
To keep finding the potential until you ignite again
and merge with the light it carries,
with the light within our o wn heart.
Let yourself rise.
So much more is meant for you.

You are not the victim of your past patterns,
you are the power to create new ones.
Within you lies everything you could ever possibly need to write a new story.

It does not matter how long that story,
that pattern,
that wound,
that thought form
has been held in your body;
you can write it out.
You can reclaim your power
in this now moment
to choose a different desire,
a different intention,
a different outcome
and invest in that reality.
You can open up
to allow all of the gifts that are already yours
and have been waiting for you since you incarnated!
Let this Now moment be the beginning.
Let go of the past by honoring its place
in the brilliance of your becoming,
but at the same time acknowledging
that you are now ready to evolve
into so much more.
Allow yourself to align with your greater potential
by using your thoughts and feelings
as the bridge to meet it,
by believing that glory,
victory,
abundance,
and ease
are also your name.

- You're always free to choose something else for yourself. -

Maybe the above is actually really the below.
And maybe the without is actually really within.
And maybe all those blessings you're seeing
outside of you,
you actually orchestrated from inside of you.
And maybe the power has been yours all along.
And maybe there's still so much more for you to discover
about the magic flowing through you.
And maybe it's time for you to remember that you can
create anything
heal anything
release anything
do anything
be anything
speak anything into existence
that you so desire
to receive.

You are the light.

Knowing you can still improve
doesn't take away
from how far you have come.

Learn to celebrate each and every overcoming.
A victory is still a victory no matter how small you might think it is.

After all, if you took away those small steps, those smaller victories,
you wouldn't be able to reach the top of the mountain.
Therefore, your victory at the top, your larger victory, is a result of
each smaller victory along the way.

Pay gratitude to your persistence and for loving yourself enough to
continue onward,
for believing that you're worthy of so much more and for following
through with receiving it.

You and your resilient heart deserve some praise.

There is no limit to how high you can rise,
to how many times you can get back up and overcome,
to how much abundance you can receive,
to how much light that can pour out from you.

But, my love, how isn't the Universe supporting you?

Isn't anything you could ever want at your fingertips?
Isn't your breath full of the Divine?
Can't you create any life that you want to receive?
Can't you encourage your heart to open up even more?
Can't your eyes learn to see more beauty?
Aren't you more than capable?
Don't you have a choice in where you want to invest your energy and what
you want to manifest?
Aren't you free?
Isn't it your divine birthright to perfectly align your energy?

Then isn't there more infinite support than you could ever need?
When you reclaim your power, you remember that this all lies in your heart
and in your hands.
That this life is a gift and you get to choose your destiny.

Everything wants to see you succeed,
but you have to allow it to.
                    It all starts inside of you.

The light is not at the end of the tunnel,
at some future destination, or at another state of being.

The light you keep looking for
has always been right inside of **you.**

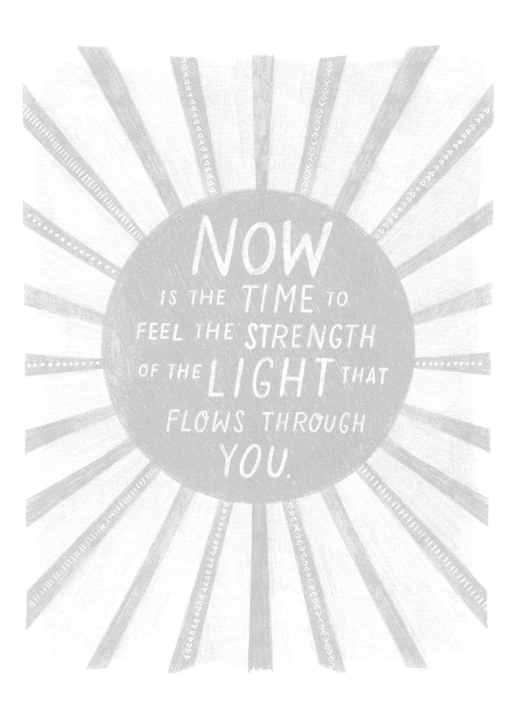

NOW IS THE TIME TO FEEL THE STRENGTH OF THE LIGHT THAT FLOWS THROUGH YOU.

Don't let yourself be treated less than,
especially by you.

You set the bar for how every other connection shows up in your
reality.
If you aren't treating yourself with the highest honor and respect, if
you aren't worshipping your own being,
then others have no example of how you'd like to be treated.
It's up to you to show them.
Choose love for every inch of yourself.
That is your divine worth.

COMMIT TO WHO YOU WANT TO BE AND LET THE REST GO.

When you're so focused on your rising,
nothing else can touch you.

Remember your power.
Remember you are unlimited.
Remember you are infinite.
Remember anything you want to be or have
is already
yours.

I BELIEVE in the POWER of MY BEING

Affirm....

I have a right to be exactly where I desire to be.
I have a right to listen to my own truth.
I have a right to forge my own path.
I have a right to reclaim my own voice, my power,
and to live authentically.

I AM allowed to be unique.
I AM allowed to go slower than others and still succeed.
I AM allowed to be joyful regardless of the circumstances.
I AM allowed to heal.
I AM allowed to outshine people.
I AM allowed to take care of myself and put my own needs first.
I AM allowed to take my time.
I AM allowed to be confused and unsure and still worthy.
I AM allowed to be me, brilliantly, and beautifully.

Stepping into your worth doesn't happen overnight.
You're unraveling thousands of ancient stories that told you
you must be small to fit into this world.
So be patient while you come undone.
While you expand once more and reach back out to merge with your
divinity.
While you realign with what is truly for you.
While you remember who you truly are.

Just be patient love.
Everything you want is coming.
Who you want to be, you already are.
You're just remembering.
You're just coming back home.

There is no one right way to heal.
There is no one path to happiness.
There is no expiration on your dreams
and there is no victory to be found in settling,
rushing,
forcing,
or living a life that isn't in alignment with your heart.

Keep your sight set on the light
and when it's your time,
when the voice in your soul is echoing so loud,
and the beat in your heart is pounding so strong,
R I S E.

Is this moment,
this choice,
this direction,
this thought-form,
these words
supporting the life you are worthy of?
Is this the future you want to create?
Does your heart feel supported?

If it doesn't, if it isn't,
there's something better out there for you.
Wait for it / Create it / Find it / Allow it / Trust in it

You are infinite potential.

I AM WORTHY

As you proclaim your worth,
you will effortlessly realign with the life,
the connections,
the blessings,
the abundance that has always been meant for you,
that has always been yours.

AFFIRM...

I feel and honor the power and divine capability of my being.

I remember I was chosen to speak up
on behalf of love.
I use my voice, my breath, my movement
to reinforce the light that I AM one with.

YOU'RE WORTHY AND ENOUGH
ON EVERY PART OF THE JOURNEY
NOT JUST ONCE YOU ARRIVE
AT WHO YOU DESIRE
TO BE

You can't settle and expect to ascend.
You can't skip the uncomfortable and expect to grow.
The uncomfortable is uncomfortable because you're diving into new
aspects of yourself.
Your soul is pushing through all the layers that aren't you.
So, have the hard conversations
when it's on behalf of your heart.
Look at what scares you and find a way to honor it.
Take the risk when your soul says Yes!
These opportunities were created just for you,
by you,
as catalysts back to the divine.
Don't run from them,
take advantage of them.

These are your blessings in disguise.
This is your magic on the rise.

Choose the risk of rejection,
choose the uncomfortable option,
choose vulnerability if it will ignite your expansion.

The highest path isn't always the easiest path,
but so many more miracles lie at the end of it.

Being brave is an act of self-love.
It's you telling the world you deserve your space in it.
It's you allowing yourself to unfold.
to be seen,
to give yourself to the world...
which is all it's ever wanted from you,
asked of you.
Just you.
Exactly the way you are.

And every time you do the "hard thing"
you face the uncomfortable,
you speak up on behalf of your heart,
you stop apologizing for being who you are,
you let yourself be seen without a mask,
you let your emotions be expressed without restriction,
you say what's on your mind without judging yourself,
you are proclaiming your worth
and the space you are deserving of in this world.
You're finally becoming one
with your vast embodiment of infinite information.
And that kind of courage doesn't come
without the Universe realigning every single thing
for your highest behalf.
So, keep reclaiming your power.
Keep reclaiming your voice.
Keep reclaiming your truth.
Keep living fearlessly
and let yourself be blessed
for finally honoring who you are
and for knowing it's enough.
Always.
It's not about being more,
it's about honoring what's already there,
who you already are.

It's not about what tore you down.
It's about what you're learning now that you have to get back up.
It's about all of the strength you're gaining
in the rising and rebuilding.

We spend so much time getting caught up in what tore us down that we forget to focus on all we're gaining in the rising and rebuilding. That's the whole point of "struggle" and triggers after all. What parts and deeper magnitudes of our self we get to rediscover and reemerge with. We get more courage, more strength, more resilience, more knowledge. We get to call on the divine, the force of grace, unconditional love, nurturance, compassion, kindness, support and healing. Don't forget to move out of your pain and see where it's actually calling you back to.

Pain is never just about pain. It's always a portal back to love.

You're allowed to let go of what no longer serves you.
You're allowed to leave things behind.
You're allowed to outgrow people, places and things.
You're allowed to constantly change and evolve and access new potential.
You're allowed to keep rising and expanding and discovering new worlds of magic within yourself.
Stop shrinking or staying small for others who refuse to grow and chase their own light.

Keep flowing forward.
Keep floating upward.

Nothing is permanent.
Everything changes.
You can rise up from anything.
You can completely recreate yourself.
You are not stuck.
You have choices.
You can think new thoughts.
You can learn new things.
You can create new habits.
All that matters is you decide today.
You honor your worth.
And you never look back.

Reprogram—-

Reprogram shame with empowerment.
Reprogram misunderstanding with gratitude.
Reprogram victimhood with sovereignty.
Reprogram lack with worth.
Reprogram destruction with creation.

When you do the thing that scares you:
You heal.
Activate new potential.
You rise.
Free your ancestry of fear.
Free your future and future generations of fear.
Strengthen your solar plexus and gut health.
Create more space in you for love.
Overcome.
Empower yourself.
Empower others.
Taste glory.
Return to your divinity.
Amplify grace.
So feel it and do it anyway.
You're worth what's on the other side.

Know that the magnitude of which
you are tested
is also the magnitude
of which
you are strengthened,
blessed,
and rewarded.

Your strength is born from your overcoming.
The "struggle" you're in
is heightening your depth
and amplifying your resilience.
Let it make you, not break you.

YOU ARE GROWING STRONGER FROM THIS

And if guilt should come,
let it come when you are living a life
that is less than what you're worthy of,
not for claiming all that you deserve.

MAY YOU ALWAYS HAVE THE COURAGE TO KEEP CHASING THE LIGHT

BECOMING

This is what you have come here for; your becoming.
To allow yourself to be constantly changing,
endlessly evolving,
expanding,
transforming,
and rising into new versions of yourself forever more.
Always continuing to discover the magic flowing through you
and going wherever it pulls you in each and every moment.
Granting yourself permission to flow with grace through your growing
pains and letting yourself rise into new potentials within yourself along
with having the courage to allow them to be shared with the world.

To allow ALL of you to be shared with the world.

There's so much beauty in the fire you've been called to walk
through.
Don't ever doubt the power, the blessings, the glory in your
becoming.

Trust in your becoming.
Trust in the process that's unfolding.
Trust in the unseen working for you.
Trust in your own power to reach glory.
Trust that this is opening your heart more.
Trust that you're rising
despite whatever appears to be weighing you down.
Trust that you're releasing what's no longer serving you.
Trust in your return back to the Divine.

YOU ARE NOT FALLING APART
YOU'RE JUST BEING PUT BACK TOGETHER
MORE RADIANT THAN EVER

You're not broken.
You're not stuck.
You're not falling apart.
You're just getting back in tune with your soul.
You're realigning with opportunities
that resonate with your new frequency.
You're fine tuning your choices,
seeing what feels good now
that you've become something stronger,
aligned,
more resilient.
You're leading more with your heart.

Yes, this can feel uncomfortable.
Yes, this can feel scary.
Yes, this can feel overwhelming and confusing,
but you are not broken.
You are whole always and forever.
You're just discovering new ways
to be a more beautiful and brighter you.

As you move through this beautiful
new season of becoming, remember
to be kind,

Your cells are releasing old stories to
the stars.

New light is weaving its way into your
new skin.

You're cracking open to fill up with
even more love, more compassion,
and more grace.

Let your journey be rewritten.
Let you potential blossom and
flourish.

Beautiful one,
You are energy.
It's your divine and physical nature to **move...**
Flowing through life.
Through emotions.
Through thoughts.
Through places.
Through vibrations.
Through connections.
So, if you're in a wonderful place,
imagine an even better one is coming to meet you.
If you're in a hard or frustrating place,
where it feels like opposition,
imagine an abundant place where the light pours in
and everything manifests with grace.
Regardless where you are,
you're going to get through this.
It's universal law.
No situation has ever remained permanent
and neither will this one.
It has to move.
You have to move forward.
And onward.
And upward.
The best is only just beginning.
The best is on its way to you.

Don't feel shame or embarrassment
towards the lessons and experiences
your soul needs
to become the best version of itself.

Don't feel like you're a burden
for the ways in which you're needed
and being called to strengthen and grow.

Don't ever feel too much for coming completely undone, unraveling,
or being burned to the ground,
in order to be rewritten,
to resurrect
and rise higher than any lifetime before.

Your becoming is your greatest gift.

It hurts because you're growing.
You're growing because your next level is ready for you.
It's scary because it's unknown.
It's unknown because you're elevating,
because you've never been at such a high level of your beingness
before.
It's lonely because you're rediscovering your sacred self,
your wholeness in its full magnitude.
And it's all worth it because you're ascending.

Because this is the journey of your homecoming.

You might not be where you desire to be,
but that doesn't mean you aren't on your way
and that it isn't coming.
Every roadblock,
every obstacle,
every detour
is gifting you with exactly what you need
to arrive at your divine destination,
with new eyes,
new strength,
and a brighter heart.
So, keep moving forward
and never doubt all of the forces
that are on your side
working so hard in the unseen
to make all you've ever wanted
be better than you can even imagine.
Surrender your fears to the universe and just keep believing.

Your new life is coming.

I know you might be tired.
You might be scared.
You might be overwhelmed or feeling weak,
but just start, my love.
Just start exactly where you are.
I promise it's enough.
The smallest step or change in direction is still incredible progress.
That means, you will no longer be exactly where you are,
that you've aligned with a new potential.
And then day by day and hour by hour
just keep moving.
It doesn't matter how quickly you move.
Just move.
Let yourself flow into something new.
Allow that shift to gain momentum by your continual action.
And celebrate every single step along the way.
That will magnetize you to your new destination even quicker
and your belief in the magic of what's to come
will take away some of the work for you
and realign you with ease,
with who you are and what you deserve.
The universe is here to help and support you,
but you have to show it you're ready and willing.
You have to allow your excitement to match your desire and destination.

Warmer days are coming, love.
With all the changes you've made,
all the flowers within that you've bloomed,
all of the old stories
you've released to the stars,
the universe is rearranging
a more perfect path for you right now.
Let it unfold in its own divine timing.
Don't get caught up in your mind
being anxious of the future
or fearing that you're stuck
or unworthy of all that you desire.
It's coming.
Stay present in your heart
and it will arrive with more grace
than you could ever imagine

This is your beginning, not your ending.
Your rise, not your fall.
From destruction comes creation.
From ash the Phoenix rises.

Take your chaos, take your broken pieces, and build your masterpiece.

Sometimes we have to come completely undone,
we have to break loose from all our dead weight,
we have to release our past identity
if we want to be new.
New breath, new look, new love, new life, new potential, new hope.

This transformation was really freedom in disguise.
Your wings have room to breathe now.
So, fly!

In the near future, these are the days
you're going to look back on.
You're going to smile.
Your heart's going to expand.
Your lungs will be full of breath.
Your tension will have subsided.
You'll be calm and relaxed.
You'll be right where you always wanted to be
doing everything you have always wanted to do.
And you're going to be so grateful.
So grateful because this big bravery
you're having to call on,
these growing pains you're enduring,
these veils you're uncovering,
this letting go,
this surrendering,
this darkness,
this imbalance
was the catalyst for your brightest light.
Trust that in order to fully rise up,
you have to step into the uncomfortable
to move into your new season.

Yes, you may still have a long way to go,
but my gosh,
have you seen how far you've come?

Shift your thoughts into acknowledgement
and celebration of how far you've come.
How many moments, how many lessons, how many emotions you didn't know
you'd make it through, but you did.
The times you wanted to give up on your dreams, but here you are...
Still stronger even if right in this moment you're being called to grow more.
Still wiser even if right in this moment you're being called to grow more.
Still more expansive even if right in this moment you're being called to grow
more.
Still lighter even if right in this moment you're being called to grow more.
The evolution never ends because Earth gifts us so many invitations to keep
becoming.
That's why we chose to come here after all.
But if you only wait to celebrate once you get to where you want to go,
you're missing the whole point of your journey.
Joy and gratitude are the most impactful and imperative parts.
So, turn your destiny into a dance.

Also, never forget that the journey is in the walking, in all of the smaller steps,
not the destination, not once you've reached the top of the mountain.
The journey is right here and now. In your being.
And you're worthy and enough right here and right now.
And you get to celebrate right here and right now because compared to
where you were yesterday or maybe even an hour ago,
that's still progress and that's still a victory.
Walking through the fire is always worth it.

This is your Homecoming.

ABOUT THE AUTHOR

 Kristen is a way shower, an example of overcoming, a strong transmitter of empowerment, and a pillar of the Ascension Flame. She is an advocate of never-ending compassion, self-acceptance and of restoring the higher consciousness and DIVINE frequencies here on Earth so that peace and unity for all may return.

She has used her soul lessons and a life-changing car accident as a portal to awakening her highest potentials. She took her darkness and allowed it to illuminate her purest light through her resilience to constantly rise as she walked forward with the remembrance of the sacred contract she made with the divine. She uses this wisdom of her multidimensionality and her understanding of the subtle realms to stand as a beacon of truth and hope for others who, too, are searching for their way back home and to process their life experiences through grace.

Kristen helps to remind us that each moment of this life is a gift despite the illusions that come with this physical reality and that our soul has divinely orchestrated the arrival of each experience and each connection on our behalf as a sacred opportunity to learn from, to grow from and to expand from. She empowers and encourages others to always choose to see through the eyes of love and with this gift she has helped to shift numerous lives to return to their power and light.

I WOULD BE HONORED TO CONNECT WITH YOU

www.youareluminous.com
www.luminousmindbodywellness.co
www.etsy.com/shop/youareluminous

Instagram + Facebook + Pinterest @youareluminous

OFFERINGS AVAILABLE

PODCAST: YOU ARE LUMINOUS
1-on-1 Self-Empowerment Sessions
Self-Empowerment, Self-love and Abundance
Affirmation card decks
Membership space with weekly support

ART BY

SHANNON CONTRERAS

SHANNONCONTRERAS
SHANNONCONTRERAS.COM

Remember that even if you don't move as fast as you'd like to, you're still making progress.

Remember that the unseen is always working FOR you.

Remember that you hold the power in each Now moment to write a new future.

Remember that your highest path isn't always your easiest path. It can sometimes feel painful, hard, and uncomfortable, but it doesn't mean it isn't exactly what you should be walking through to carry you to your most beautiful destination yet.

Remember that growth comes from overcoming.

Remember that you can go slow, question yourself and your path, change your mind, and still succeed.

Remember that your healing might take longer than others and that's perfect.

Remember that you can't have a new beginning without an ending or a change in direction.

Remember that magic can't be rushed and you'll get there right when you're meant to be.

Made in the USA
Middletown, DE
28 February 2020